Images Around Birkenshaw

A Collection of Photographs - 2020

Paul D. Foy, MA, MMath (Cantab), PhD

This book contains photographs in and around Birkenshaw, West Yorkshire, UK. They are accompanied by annotations. Included are areas of South Bradford, South Leeds and North Kirklees Metropolitan areas, as well as Birkenshaw itself.

Published in 2020 by
Paul D. Foy

First Edition
Printed by
Solopress UK

ISBN 978-1-5272-8005-2

© Paul D. Foy

Front Cover: Greeting sign at the Halfway House, showing the headquarters of West Yorkshire Fire & Rescue Service, probably Birkenshaw's biggest employer.

Acknowledgement

The author appreciates the help given by my mother and father in proof-reading and for making suggestions throughout the writing and gathering of photographs for this book.

Contents

1. INTRODUCTION 9
2. BIRKENSHAW 11
3. BIRSTALL, BATLEY AND GOMERSAL 51
4. CLECKHEATON, LIVERSEDGE AND
   HECKMONDWIKE 81
5. DUDLEY HILL, BOWLING, BIERLEY AND
   HOLME WOOD 103
6. TONG AND DRIGHLINGTON 117
7. OAKENSHAW, WYKE, LOW MOOR AND WIBSEY 127
8. REFERENCES 145

1 Introduction

Birkenshaw lies at the centre of West Yorkshire, but being a new village, without apparently a Manor, has struggled recently to form an identity. Ironically, there are however several so named 'Manor Houses' in Birkenshaw. It is hoped that this collection of images taken in the second half of 2020, of present day features of Birkenshaw and its surroundings, will help to correct this. The images are of modern features and establishments, together with older historical ones, and their relationship to the present. As well as Birkenshaw itself there are images of the surrounding towns, villages and suburbs to the North, South, East and West.

To the North and North East we have the suburbs of Bradford which were themselves, before being amalgamated into the city, often separate hamlets. There is Oakenshaw, Low Moor, Bierley, Bolling, Dudley Hill and Holme Wood.

To the West and North West we have Tong and Drighlington, Tong being considered as part of Bradford and Drighlington as part of Leeds.

To the South we have the towns which together with Birkenshaw constituted the administrative region of Spen Valley. That is Gomersal, Cleckheaton, Liversedge and Heckmondwike. In addition, Birstall and Batley, which together with Spen Valley forms the parliamentary constituency of Batley & Spen.

On all sides there are old manor houses dating back to William the Conqueror and beyond. Birkenshaw itself is something of a newcomer.

Nowadays, Birkenshaw is considered as part of the administrative region of Kirklees. It is indeed the Northern tip of this region, which also includes the large town of Huddersfield to the South.

Residents of Birkenshaw often travel to all of these areas for both work and pleasure, as well as to the centres of the larger cities of Leeds and Bradford.

This account is my own personal collection of photographs, in and around Birkenshaw, from someone who was born in Birkenshaw in 1964. Having spent my formative years until 1990, based in Birkenshaw, I then went to live in Dursley, Gloucestershire, to work, for 30 years before returning to live again in Birkenshaw in 2020. I am thus able to compare and contrast the very old, the old, and the new. The collection of images was gathered in the second half of 2020.

2 Birkenshaw

The name Birkenshaw means Birch-Grove or clearing and is Anglo Saxon in origin, these probably being the earliest settlers. Indeed somewhere around AD620 an immigrant called Guthmer probably settled in the area, cleared some land and built a fortified house - 'Guthmer's Halh'. Hence we have the name Gomersal. Why this was not at Birkenshaw is probably because the land or its aspect was not as attractive - these are the usual reasons for early settling in a place.
There is an entry in the Oxford Dictionary of Place Names of a place *Birkenschawe* with the date 1274, and indeed court rolls

of the period indicated that such a place yielded tax to an Ilbert de Lacy, Knight of Pontefract. It must be remembered that from the conquest of England by William the Conqueror and the Normans in 1066, vast tracts of land in the North (and South) were given to William's supporters (military men or Knights). Ilbert de Lacy was one such follower. People were granted permission to live within a Knight's lands at varying levels of servitude, consequent on them paying taxes in money or kind (e.g. labour, chickens, military service etc.). For example they could be yeomen owning the freehold of a property, or at the lowest level slaves, with no property rights, at the total beck and call of their masters. The Knights themselves paid taxes to the King (or Queen). Thus, the English class system was established.

Many of the original Saxon English landholders (Thanes) had their manorial system taken over and subjected to the oversight of the new conquerors.

The introductory image shows the main street in Birkenshaw as it is today (2020). This is one of the main roads through the area - Bradford Road. Note the numbers of cars in the image. This is one of the features of the photographs in this collection. Cars are one of the ubiquitous features of this age. Indeed it would often be impossible to wait to obtain a picture which was free of some car or other.

This is the Manor House at the junction of Town Street, Station Lane and Mill Lane. It is one of the oldest houses in Birkenshaw. At the time of taking the photograph it was a hair and beauty spa but has now reverted to being a private residence.

In the 18th and 19th centuries conditions for children were poor. They were expected (indeed needed) to work - down mines, in cloth mills or on the land. Education for young children of the working classes was almost non-existent and what there was had to be paid for. Around 1840 parliament allocated money to encourage local authorities to provide some schooling. Thus in 1838, with the campaigning of Reverend Henry John Smith of St. Paul's Church Birkenshaw, the first Birkenshaw National School was built to provide elementary education. The Law followed the money and in 1870 the Elementary Education Act was passed making the provision of elementary education compulsory.

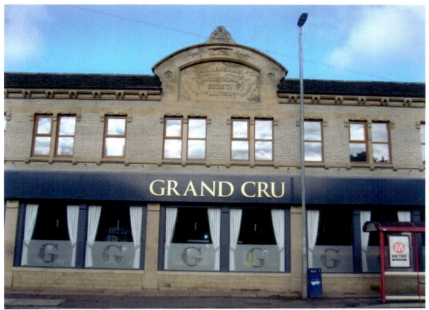

With the introduction of the Education Reform Act in 1870, thought was also given to easing the plight of, and providing for the education of the adult working classes. With that in mind Mechanics Institutes and Industrial Societies were formed. These provided (often for a modest fee) adult education and perhaps entertainment services. Birkenshaw was relatively late in providing such provision and this building stems from 1887. It has had many uses since including carpet shop and cooperative food store and presently houses a restaurant and children's nursery.

This is a view of Tong Moor looking to the North-East off Station Lane - height 210m. This is urban green space - believed to have been given to the authorities, by a local landowner, to remain undeveloped, in perpetuity. It is a fairly ancient moor and perhaps indicates why this area was not attractive to the very early settlers. The land here is not good for arable crops, indicating why early settlers had to supplement their income by spinning wool, as well as gathering coal for heating from the exposed coal seams. The track down the middle is part of an ancient packhorse track linking Westgate Hill and Drighlington.

Birkenshaw CE Primary School is situated on Station Lane. This school replaced the old National School.

Sherburn House situated on Station Lane, opposite the primary school. This house was built in the 20th century.

Here is a view looking South East from Station Lane, in the opposite direction to Tong Moor. Emley Moor television and radio mast is just visible in the middle of the picture.

This is an old house on the junction of Old Lane, Station Lane, Mill Lane and Town Street. There may well have been a toll house on or near this spot at one time.

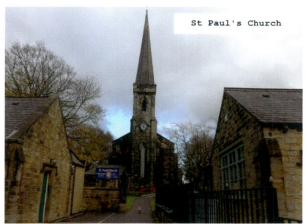

Originally Birkenshaw's religious needs were met by the church of the large parish of Birstall (as were other settlements in the area). As populations grew during the industrial period it was decided to form a separate chapelry. St. Paul's Church Birkenshaw (including East Bierley) was therefore consecrated in 1831.

Here is Birkenshaw's graveyard, behind St.Paul's Church. This was established on 3 acres of land donated by the Birkenshaw industrialist William Ackroyd.

Medieval England with its land owning hierarchy was largely Catholic. Anglicanism was the dominant religion practised in England (the Church of England), after the split with Henry VIII. Methodism is a branch of Christianity, often understood as being what is known as Protestantism, which was started by John Wesley. It was considered a rebellious doctrine by the authorities initially, though it was popular in this region. It was followed by many prominent industrialists who gave money to found the many such churches in the area. This is Birkenshaw's currently only surviving Methodist church (there were once several). It lies on Bradford Road, near Furnace Lane.

This is the Halfway House public house on the crossroads of the A58 Leeds to Halifax road and the A651 Bradford to Heckmondwike road. Again, Birkenshaw is at the centre of things. There was once a tramway from Bradford to the Halfway House, and another one from the Halfway House to Dewsbury and Heckmondwike. Because these were run by different companies, the gauges were not the same, so onward travellers had to change! Hence the need for a resting place. Indeed, around 1900 a toilet was built on the spot where the photographer is standing in this picture. There was never a tramway on the A58. It was only used by stagecoaches and then, as today, by motorbuses and cars.

Bank view - modern housing on Bradford Road, next to the Methodist church, built in the 21st century.

This is Threelands - modern housing on Bradford Road opposite the Methodist church. It was originally the grounds of a private house of the same name, subsequently taken over as the West Yorkshire Ambulance Service Headquarters.

Before 1780 Birkenshaw was just a collection of scattered farmsteads, tending the land and perhaps spinning their own wool. Then there was the development of iron and coal production. There were many foundries in the area (both large and small): Low Moor, Bowling, Bierley, and Birstall. The one in Birkenshaw was started by the industrialist John Emmet, and was based behind the Methodist church, and existed from 1788 to 1811. When the foundry closed the workers would transfer to Low Moor or Bowling, much as workers re-locate today. Today, the only relic of it is the unmetalled private road, Furnace Lane, off Bradford Road, on the right of this old house.

A collection of old houses on Bradford Road opposite Furnace Lane, built to house workers at the foundry. The small middle one was once a pub known as 'The Wellington' - no longer used, once the foundry closed.

The Hawthornes retirement flats - built in 2003, off Bradford Road opposite Bank View.

One of the dominant textile concerns in Birkenshaw was the Oddy family. James Oddy (the son) built this row of terrace houses in 1903. Southfield Terrace was built for his workers in Moorlands Mill nearby.

Moorlands Square, off Moorlands Road, was also built by the Oddy's for the workers at Moorlands Mill nearby. During restoration the midden (running down the centre) was replaced by a car park (a sign of the times). The original James Oddy lived at Lapwater Hall on the A650 Wakefield Road near Cross Lane End. His sons and their offspring lived at two residences near Moorlands Mills - Moorlands Hall and Moorville. Both of these have been replaced by more modern housing. Their names have given rise to the names of streets in the area, as was and still is common practice.

Coming right up to date we have the new housing scheme at Heathfield Farm, adjacent to the M62 off the A58. Note the modern (cheaper) building material - brick.

More new houses, some still under construction, at Heathfield Farm. The name 'Emmet' on a street gives reference to one of Birkenshaw's early industrialists.

The Heathfield Farm family orientated restaurant, a modern dining trend.

View of the extensive Blue Hills Farm. It derives its name from the fact that it is thought to have been the recipient of blue shale waste from the foundry in Furnace Lane (perhaps via some form of canal).

This is Birkenshaw's community library at Sparrow Park at the Halfway House roundabout. The library is maintained by the Birkenshaw Village Association.

The M62, crossing Bradford Road here, is now effectively the boundary of Birkenshaw to the South. The 1974, IRA M62 coach bombing, which killed 12 people, happened here.

Birkenshaw allotments

Allotments were established when common lands were no longer left for the use of ordinary people. They became popular amongst working families during the industrialisation of the 19th and early 20th centuries. During the two World Wars there were about 1.5 million in use. Birkenshaw once had several allotment sites. There are now only two sites left: on Station Lane and at Birkenshaw Bottoms. This allotment is on the Station Lane plot, the whole site having vehicular access from Old Lane. Once popular amongst working families for growing food, they are now seen as a leisure activity. Their numbers have dwindled because of the lack of interest and the need (and remuneration to the Council!) for housing.

East Bierley is a village to the North of Birkenshaw, which well over a hundred years ago was surrounded by mine workings (both open cast and underground). Because of the poor nature of the land there is no evidence of open field farming. The village's poor transport links probably prevented the industrialisation that occurred along Tong Street and Dudley Hill. At the turn of the 20th century most people would be employed in the mines, or in Moorlands Mill (owned by the Oddy family). After the First World War, the Oddy's built a memorial hall for the village which is now St. Luke's Church and Hall. Today, the village has a rural feel to it. This notice board, by the pond, lists the various sights in the village.

These are the village stocks - quaint objects, like the ducking stool (!), of punishment. Whether they were, in reality, used a lot here, is debateable.

Here is the ancient East Bierley pond. One hot summer when the pond dried up, the ducks were taken away, and on return they found that they had been provided with nesting boxes.

This is a sign of the times - the Methodist chapel in East Bierley converted into flats, to meet the ever increasing need for housing.

The picture shows typical miners' cottages on South View Road, East Bierley. That is, single storey two or three room stone cottages. Many of the inhabitants of East Bierley would have worked in the mines.

Here we have a tradesman at work in Birkenshaw.

The picture shows the Arriva bus service in Birkenshaw.

Town houses on Bradford Road, by the senior school.

The picture shows flowers adjacent to the roundabout, at the Halfway House. They are looked after by the Birkenshaw Village Association.

The picture shows a view of the BBG Academy 'free' school in Birkenshaw, which educates pupils up to 16 years old. Originally designed by the disgraced architect John Poulson, this was once a middle school (I attended) only educating between 9 to 13 years old pupils.

Here is a view of the old WW2 air raid shelter in Sparrow Park, off the Halfway House roundabout.

Stone was once the dominant building material in the Bradford region and many old walls were built from it. This one on North View Road is in need of some repair!

This is a traditional nursery business on North View Road. Many of these traditional undertakings have unfortunately been replaced by larger garden centres. The growing of food is done more for leisure than need nowadays.

The old school house on Westgate Hill Street - now converted into flats - the need for good housing with the ever expanding population becomes more and more acute.

Estate agents have sprung up everywhere to cater for more changes of accommodation, and a greater supply of flats and houses. Beauty shops (on the right) cater for increased time and money to adorn oneself.

The development of Southern Birkenshaw occurred in what is now known as Birkenshaw Bottoms. This is a row of period stone houses on Moor Lane that is over 120 years old. They were probably built for the workers of William Ackroyd's worsted mill (from 1832) that occupied what is now Kingsley housing estate.

This is Gomersal Park Hotel and restaurant, on Moor Lane. It was originally Moor Lane House, which in the 19th century was owned by the Wormald family.

Here is the Fleece Inn, one of Birkenshaw's three public houses.

The need to try on clothes before purchase, as well as the vicissitudes of fashion, has meant that small independent clothes shops, like Readmans, can survive the onslaught of internet shopping.

Petrol stations, like this one on Wakefield Road, fuel the ubiquitous cars. A modern trend is the provision of a grocers/newsagent on the forecourt.

For many years this building was Birkenshaw's Post Office. It is now a coffee shop.

Traditional housing on Town Street. The house on the right was once a draper's shop. This was when the making of one's clothes was popular.

These flats, on Town Street, were once a butcher's shop, before independent butchers lost trade to the big supermarkets.

A supermarket from one of the big chains - the Coop.

Birkenshaw's last remaining independent butcher. The establishment is renowned for its pies and commitment to local customers.

These are growth industries at the time of writing - a barbers and a beauty salon.

The pharmacy attached to the Birkenshaw Health Centre, on Town Street.

Another growth industry - personal care for the elderly, replaced what was once a grocer's shop.

This is a view of the haulage distribution depot on the location of Birkenshaw's original rail station, off Cross Lane. Transport and distribution hubs are a feature of the times.

A house in Station Lane bedecked in Halloween attire. The celebration of Halloween, including its commercial exploitation, is a more American tradition, which is becoming popular in the area. This picture reminds me of how the residents in the farmsteads used to hang cloth out to dry on tenter frames.

Here is a picture of The Nawaab Indian restaurant at Lapwater Hall, which was once the Oddy's residence. The original hall is just visible. The term 'Nawaab' refers to a (usually Muslim) ruler of a province, and perhaps befits the residence of Birkenshaw's prominent industrialist. Members of the East Asian community, were invited here as cheap labour, for the mills, in the 50's. This was in contrast to their use as labour in India during British rule. They are now the providers of food in this community, as their original form of labour is no longer considered viable (the work often being done more cheaply in East Asia!).

This is a view of The George IV public house in the centre of Birkenshaw village. Birkenshaw would be nothing were it not for its roads. Originally it was little more than a settlement off a road from Birstall to Westgate Hill. Then in the 17th century came the turnpike roads (that is roads whose construction and use were funded by levying tolls, collected on the roads at turnpikes). The George IV was built to cater for the turnpike road from Holme Lane End via Westgate Hill, Cross Lane, Station Lane, Town Street and on to Heckmondwike. Later on a more direct route was constructed from Town Street to Westgate Hill with a toll at Bierley Bar. This section of Bradford road no doubt heralded the construction of the various mills along this stretch of the road. Another Turnpike Trust constructed the road from Leeds to Halifax passing by the Halfway House.

Christmas lights originated as a pagan celebration (fires, the lighting of candles etc.) to mark the lengthening of the days after the winter solstice. They were then incorporated into the Christian celebration of Christmas. The first electric Christmas lights to be displayed were on the Savoy Hotel in London in 1881. Today the decorating of houses, around Christmas, with fairy lights is widespread. This is a short row of privately owned houses, bedecked in illuminations, in Threelands, Birkenshaw.

There has been a tradition of a display of seasonal lights in Birkenshaw for several years during the Christmas and winter solstice periods. The present one is organised by the Birkenshaw Village Association. It is an attractive sight. This is a view of the lights looking North on Bradford Road.

This is a view of the lights, near the same spot, looking South on Bradford Road.

3 Birstall, Batley and Gomersal

These areas to the South of Birkenshaw contain some of the discernibly oldest settlements. Birstall is derived from old English '*byrh*' (place) and *stall* (fortified), and was probably the fortified enclave of '*Guthmar's Hahl*', parts of it being on high ground. There are relics of Roman and Anglo-Saxon origin in the area and indeed an inspection of old maps reveals that until fairly recently the ancient open field system of farming was practised in Gomersal. Although there is no mention of Birstall in the Doomesday book it is likely that Birstall (perhaps the church or a mill by it) became the centre of life in the area.

Soon afterwards, Oakwell Hall seems to have been the Manor House of the region. Batley was under the control of Ilbert de Lacey, Lord of the Manor at Batley Hall, one of the Conquerors followers.

However as with other areas around Birkenshaw, it is the advent of industrialisation, and in particular the development of the textile industries and coal mining, that left its mark on the area. Gomersal was instrumental in weaving quite early and the advent and timing of industrialisation is mirrored in the buildings of this area. Batley became famous for the processing of recycled cloth with the shoddy and mungo trades. At the turn of the 20th century there were mills and coal mines in all the three districts. The mill owners in Batley and Gomersal built a substantial number of houses for themselves and for their workers (for example, the houses down Oxford Road, Gomersal).

The opening picture is a photograph of Hill Top crossroads, Gomersal, looking North along Oxford Road.

Birstall War Memorial opposite St Peter's Church, off Kirkgate, Birstall. Almost every community in the area has a war memorial of some sort, commemorating those killed in the 1st and 2nd World Wars.

A sign of the times - a discarded face mask, near St Peter's Church, Birstall. These were used for protection against Coronavirus, during most of 2020.

This is a picture of the old National School, on Low Lane, Birstall. This was built in 1818 and is now being used as business premises.

Here we have Longbottom Dam, off Kirkgate, Birstall. Originally the mill pond of a dye works, and perhaps, earlier, that of the Manor's mill. It is now a pleasant area for fishermen.

St Peter's Church, Birstall. There was no mention of this church or Birstall in the Doomesday Book (1086) - it usually mentioned landowners. However there is evidence of Norman features in the church, and the church itself was built soon after. Birstall church like other early churches of the period served a variety of functions as well as religious ones. The mill pond and mill next to the church was probably used by the community (perhaps paying usage rents to the church). The church may have been used as a meeting place. In addition, it can be considered to be Gomersal's church, as this community did not have a church until the 19th century.

This is The Black Bull Inn, opposite St. Peter's Church, Birstall. This is an old inn, dating from the 17th century though the front facade is from around 1800. The inn would have served people coming from Gomersal to the church, as well as those on several old routes in the area. Pubs used to serve many roles in the community - this one was a magistrate's court and a local election polling station, as well as a meeting place.

These houses are on Moat Hill, to the North of the centre of Birstall. When Birstall was originally settled, as a fortified residence, it would have been to the North of the present town centre, up the Leeds Road. The term Moat originates from an ancient word meaning to meet for official business. Indeed the term meeting in a corporate or business sense may well originate from this word. Birstall was among only a handful of places in Anglo-Saxon Britain where official meetings took place. This meeting place like so many other ancient relics of the region is now a housing estate.

This is a statue of Joseph Priestley, scientist, in Market Square, Birstall. He was credited with the discovery of Oxygen. He was born near Field Head Lane in a house now demolished, and spent much of his time in the area.

Here is a view of the lake at Wilton Park, with wildlife, off Bradford Road. Wilton Park was opened by the corporation of Batley in 1909. It comprises the grounds of George Sheard's mansion, and some of the lands of Earl Winton, a major landowner in the district.

This is The Butterfly House at Wilton Park, Batley.

View from the Butterfly House looking towards Upper Batley.

At the turn of the last century there was a heavy density of railway lines. These are now almost all gone. This is a disused bridge in Wilton Park which carried the Birstall branch of the London & North Western Railway line.

This building was originally a mansion built for George Sheard, a mill owner. When George Sheard died it was acquired by the state and converted into a museum by William Bagshaw, the first curator. It lies at the entrance to the park off Woodlands Road.

This, Batley's town hall, was erected in 1853 at the height of the industrial textile trade. Batley is an ancient town. It was mentioned in the Doomesday book as 'Bateleie' and was granted to Ilbert de Lacy by the Conqueror. The Manor House, occupying a commanding position, as expected from an old house, is now a nursing home on what is Old Hall Lane. The Manor House passed into the ownership of the de Batleys.

'The Mill', on Bradford Road, Batley, is one of the UK's largest converted mill retail outlets.

Talbot Street Batley. Traditional stone terrace housing, built for mill workers over 100 years ago, has been tastefully modernised.

Field Lane, Junior, Infant & Nursery school built on Albion Street, Batley. The school is over 130 years old and serves a multi-cultural intake, from the surrounding streets.

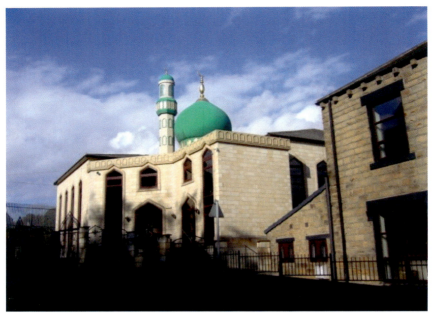

This picture shows a mosque on Taylor Street, for those of the Muslim faith amongst the new settlers. In the first half of the 19th century there were many strikes in the mills (wages and conditions no doubt). This led the owners to import cheap labour from Ireland. They and their descendants settled permanently. In the 1950's there was again a *need* for cheap labour. People from South East Asia were encouraged to settle.

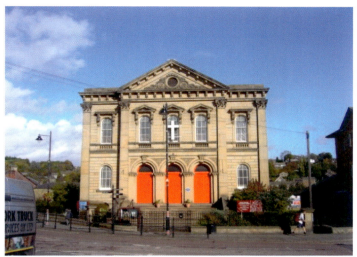

The Central Methodist Church on Commercial Street, Batley, was opened in 1870 and reflected the popularity of Methodism in both Batley and the wider area.

Here is a picture of Batley Baths in Cambridge Street.

Fox's Biscuits was founded by Michael Spedding, and is shown in its premises on Wellington Street. The Company has recently been acquired by the Italian Group Ferrero.

Newsagents have for a while been popular. This one is on Commercial Street, Batley.

This is Batley War Memorial in Memorial Park, on Cambridge Street.

Batley Grammar School on Carlinghow Hill, was founded in 1612. There was a choice of attending here from Birkenshaw, but I chose to attend Whitcliffe Mount Comprehensive School instead.

The office of the local MP (2020) is situated at Hill Top, Oxford Road, Gomersal.

A podiatrist situated at Hill Top, Oxford Road, Gomersal.

This is Gomersal's original workhouse on Muffit Lane. It was built in the 18th century to ease the problems of poor people in the district, by providing them with food and shelter in exchange for work. Originally it housed women and children - they could be sent down the mines to 'hurry', or even be bought by the mine. When modern times arrived, the 1842 Mining Act forbade women and children from working underground - and a man had to be at least 10 years of age - an early inequality! The workhouse was considered the last resort.

This is modern housing on Popeley Rise off Muffit Lane, which was built on the land of Popeley farm. The Popeley's are an ancient Gomersal family (there was a grant of land to a 'Johanne de Papelaia' soon after The Conquest). Whether the name comes from the place or vice-versa I don't know - anyway the two are related as usual. Unlike in the de Papelaia days someone is now responsible for taking the rubbish away - witness a modern dustbin lorry.

St Mary's Church, Gomersal, built in 1851. A church for Gomersal arrived relatively late as before this St Peter's in Birstall was the one frequented.

The Bulls Head Inn situated on Quarry Road, Gomersal. Pubs played an integral part in the community, being meeting places, socialising places, eating places. One of the original owners here was a blacksmith.

The Red House, situated on Oxford Road, Gomersal. This house was inhabited by the Taylors (weavers and mill owners) from the 16th century. It was probably sold to a family of that name by The Lord of The Manor at Oakwell, and it was in the possession of this family for hundreds of years. Mary Taylor was a school friend of Charlotte Bronte, the author. There may well have been sub-manors at Gomersal - there are so many big old houses. Note the substantial stone wall surrounding the property - these walls and barriers are unfortunately not a new phenomenon (perhaps now they are used to shield from traffic). There are records of, in 1611, The Lord at Oakwell Hall, paying £39 to construct a wall surrounding his property. This is a phenomenal sum - equivalent to over £750,000 in today's money (39×1.025^{400}).

Gomersal Public Hall, Oxford Road, opened in 1852, as a Mechanics Institute, to provide education of a non-sectarian nature.

This is modern housing on Quarry Road, opposite The Black Bull. It was built in 1978, as the inscription on the bottom right wall shows.

Peel House on Knowles Lane, Gomersal. The original Richard Peel, a yeoman clothier, acquired the house from the Lord of The Manor at Oakwell Hall in the 17th century.

Here we have old houses off Moor Lane, Gomersal. They are unusual, in that they are at right angles to the road. It may be that, like the workhouse, the residents worked communally, with goods entering from the door on the first floor on Moor Lane.

This is the Moravian church on Quarry Lane, Gomersal. The Moravians were a German, Methodist sect. There were many Protestant sects in the area during both the early and late industrial periods. The Moravian church in Little Gomersal was one of the earliest settlements in England, dating from 1751.

Pollard House is now a series of luxury flats. Once one of Gomersal's grandest houses it was probably initially tenanted by a person of the name of Pollard (there were Pollards in Birstall and Tong) at the call of the Lord of The Manor at Oakwell. Subsequently it became the home and headquarters of Thomas Burnley's business. Prior to factories, manufacturing operations were often based around big houses and their grounds. This was the case here before Burnley built his mill on Spen Lane.
.

Queens Court - a modern flat complex on Moor Lane, Gomersal. As Prince Charles has remarked, on similar buildings, this one seems strangely out of place in terms of location, style and functionality. The front entrance of the building is located in a space between two houses, whilst the building itself occupies a space at the rear, partially behind houses. However, in the developer's defence, there are several strange, juxtaposed buildings along Moor Lane (one has been previously mentioned). In addition, 12 households have been accommodated.

Gomersal Cricket Ground. Cricket has always been popular throughout the region and there are many cricket grounds. It was a place where people of all classes mixed for recreation.

Burnley's Mill has now gone - it has been replaced by modern housing built very recently. This is on Burnleys Mill Road, off Spen Lane.

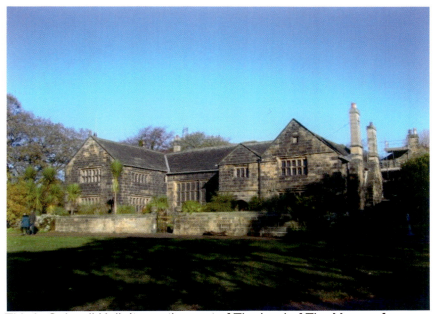

This is Oakwell Hall. It was the seat of The Lord of The Manor of Gomersal and beyond; the present building probably originating in the 16th century. However the early Lords of the Manor seem to reflect the worst of this medieval class system. The early incumbent (a Henry Batt) was notorious for avariciously trying to advance himself in money and lands at every opportunity. He would, for example, insist on onerous terms for the grinding of corn at the manorial mill, or engage in deed and accession falsification. No wonder he needed such a big wall around his property. We have an early capitalist in another guise?

This is a remnant of the bridge of the London & North Western Railway. The Heaton Lodge & Wortley railway line crossed Bradford Road adjacent to Moor Lane.

4   Cleckheaton, Liversedge and Heckmondwike

These three towns are today a short drive or bus trip away from Birkenshaw, and are frequented by residents of Birkenshaw for shopping and recreational purposes. This may not have been the case before the advent of cars or motorbuses as there was no natural tramway or train connection. They now constitute what is typically regarded as Spen Valley even though Birkenshaw and Gomersal are nowadays included in this designation. The name is chosen because these towns'

locations and industries are based upon the river Spen, which emanates in Toftshaw near Bierley in Bradford and flows on down, consecutively, through Cleckheation, Liversedge and Heckmondwike.

The oldest areas to be settled were on the slopes around Liversedge away from the boggy marshes of the Spen. Open field farming and wool spinning would have been practised by the Saxons and the early Norman conquerors, practising the feudal system mentioned in the introduction. Edward III encouraged the settling of Flemish cloth experts including one Thomas Blanquette, from which the word 'blanket' has its origin. These were the founders of what was to become the dominant industry of the region, characterising it as the 'Heavy Woollen District'. At the height of the region's industry, there were numerous mills in the area, practising all forms of cloth manufacture. In addition, there were also numerous carpet manufacturers, coal mines, dye works, (iron) foundries and other related industries. Many used the waters of the Spen. Coal was used to produce steam to drive the machinery following the industrial revolution of the 19th century. Before that, its abundance in the region meant it could be used in heating and cooking on the farmsteads.

The towns grew and developed. However today, many of the cloth and woollen mills are demolished or have been converted into housing.

The opening picture shows the main street through Cleckheaton, with the town hall visible on the right. There is a full view in the next picture.

Cleckheaton Town Hall, opened in 1892. The building was originally conceived to provide council offices, a council chamber, and a 500 seat public hall.

This is Royds Park on the Bradford Road from Cleckheaton to Heckmondwike. It was originally opposite Rawfolds Mill, owned by William Cartwright, which suffered a Luddite attack.

Cleckheaton library opened in the 1930s. This is the view of the rear of the building, which due to Coronavirus precautions, is currently the main exit.

Princess Mary's athletic track and stadium. This was one of the first synthetic (all weather) athletics tracks in the North and should have been the jewel in the crown of Spen's sporting facilities. However the site seems not to have reached its full potential.

This is a photo of Heckmondwike War Memorial. This commemorates WW1, WW2 and the Korean War.

Almshouses situated in New Road East, Scholes, Cleckheaton. Almshouses were used before drawing a pension became common, to support those who had been in employment but were now too old or sick to work.

This is a view of St Philip & St James Church, at Town Gate, Scholes.

Baden-Powell Hall on Town Gate, Scholes This was built in 1879, and is now a house and apartments.

There is a Coop supermarket store in Scholes, shown here.

Here we have a sign of the times - a car dealer. Stoneacre is at the junction of Bradford Road and Whitechapel Road, Cleckheaton.

This is the workshop of Stoneacre car dealer, Cleckheaton.

This is Whitcliffe Mount Comprehensive School, Cleckheaton, which I attended. Such schools arose out of the Mechanics Institutes of the 19th Century. Whitcliffe Mount senior school was founded early in the 20th century. The present building is very modern.

The Walton Cross at Hartshead Moorside. The picture shows the decoration on it. It is one of the few Anglo Saxon relics in the region. Thought to have been originally 5m tall, it may have been a preaching cross or a way marker as in its commanding position it would have been visible for miles.

This is a view of the Walkers Arms pub, Scholes Lane, Scholes. It was originally (from 1880) a tied pub of Richard Whitaker & Sons Ltd., brewer, Halifax.

A cycle shop on Westgate, Cleckheaton. Cycling has always struggled to compete with the motor car, due to the hilly terrain and the volume of traffic. However the recently opened National Cycle Route 66, from Hull to Manchester, runs through Cleckheaton.

Heckmondwike has always had an independent spirit and was originally not regarded as part of Spen Valley. It finally stopped generating its own electricity in 1924. This building is part of the original power station, in Bath Road.

This is a photographic shop on Market Street, Heckmondwike. Photos (for weddings, special occasions etc.) are popular, even today.

A building on Albion Street, Heckmondwike, which was originally a Christian chapel, has been converted to a mosque. 'Kanzul Iman' is one of the translations of the Qur'an into the Urdu language.

Here is another mosque in Victoria Street, Heckmondwike. The building was originally a school.

This is the Masonic Hall on Market Street, Heckmondwike. Large halls like this were often used as meeting places for many disparate events - even the town council!

This is the library in Market Street, Heckmondwike.

This clock in Heckmondwike's town centre was erected in 1863 to celebrate the marriage of the Prince of Wales and Princess Alexandra of Denmark. The inner workings of the clock are more recent.

This is Cleckheaton Post Office on Greenside, opposite the Memorial Park. The post is still an important means of communication although it is facing stiff competition from e-mail, instant messaging and other digital technologies.

Substantial stone housing on Pyenot Hall Lane, on the approach to Pyenot Hall. The housing is at least 100 years old.

Pyenot Hall was built around 1785, by Henry Birkby an industrialist who helped develop Cleckheaton's card making business (cards were used in combing wool or cotton and were originally meticulously handmade). He lived in the hall for a time before it became headquarters for the Pyenot Hall Card Works and also The Pyenot Wire Works across the road. The hall itself was demolished in the 1990's and Barratt Homes, the builders, built an estate of houses of which this is one. The lion shown in the garden of this house, bedecked the entrance gates to Pyenot Hall, and was thought to be a symbol of good luck.

This is an image of The Marsh public house on Bradford Road. Here the inquest to the Marsh Mill tragedy was held. This accident occurred in 1892 when a 500 ton chimney collapsed into the factory.

Cleckheaton Fire Station off Hightown Road. At the time of writing (2020) this station was due to be relocated to Birkenshaw.

This is the entrance to the indoor market in Cleckheaton. Outdoor markets are now less common than they used to be. However, indoor ones can still compete with the internet for value, convenience and hard to find articles.

This is a view of houses on Bridon Way, Cleckheaton. This estate replaced the house and grounds of Pyenot Hall.

This is Cleckheaton bus station. Bus travel is still popular today but suffers due to the convenience and affordability of the private car.

This is a nursery next to new housing on the site of Marsh Mills. These days many women work during their child bearing years and nurseries have sprung up to look after the young children during work times.

Liversedge Hall, shown here, on Liversedge Hall Lane, is one of the oldest residences in the region. It is likely that the area of the land was once held by a Saxon Thane and following the conquest was given to the de Liversedges. When there were fewer people, individual's names (particularly their surnames) were derived from where they originated, and then later from their occupation. The meaning of Liversedge itself has various conjectures: the Saxon *Leofric's edge* or boundary, the Celtic word *Levers* signifying great whilst edge refers to a range of hills, or the Anglo-Saxon words *Liver* and *Secg* signifying a reed like plant etc. The house and lands themselves were held by a succession of Lords of the Manor.

We have a view of fairly modern housing on Lower Hall Close off the A649, Halifax Road. This is on the site of what was Lower Hall House.

Joseph Bilton, a wealthy business man from Leeds, built Healds Hall in 1764. It has been home to a succession of notable residents and is now a hotel, restaurant and function venue.

This is The Savile Arms, Hunsworth Lane, Hunsworth. Named after one of the Lords of the Manor in the Middle Ages, his lands originally a gift from Ilbert de Lacy.

This is a picture of The Shears Inn, Liversedge. The Luddites gathered here on the evening of their unsuccessful attack to destroy the equipment at Cartwright's mill.

Liversedge was once a more prominent place and had a Town Hall, shown here. However this has now been converted into flats.

Here we have a traditional road sign in Westgate, Cleckheaton. Note the yellow clothes recycling caddy.

5 Dudley Hill, Bowling, Bierley and Holme Wood

This area (the roads of which one must drive through to access Bradford city centre from Birkenshaw) has experienced some of the most profound changes physically in the last few centuries. At the start of the 17th century Birkenshaw and its surroundings were a collection of scattered farmsteads. They were transformed, with the advent of coal mining and the iron and textile industry, into one of heavy industry.

Along Tong Street were all the mills, dye works and iron works. There was the Bowling Iron works bringing coal and iron ore from what is now Bolling Hall Park and the Tong estate. There were numerous coal pits around East Bierley, and on what is now the Holme Wood estate. In addition there was the large Tong estate to the South East. Mixed in with all this are the houses for the workers of all the enterprises, who unlike the factory owners had to live amidst the noise and pollution of the industries.

Then in the 1950's the Holme Wood estate was created to solve the problem of poor housing, inadequate roads, and to provide for newer, knowledge based industries. To this day the jury is out on the success of this.

The South of this area contains, on a position commanding Bradford, one of the oldest Houses in Bradford - Bolling Hall Manor.

The opening picture shows Tong Street near its junction with Holme Lane.

Tyre and exhaust fitting while you wait is possible, on Tong Street, Dudley Hill. The operators here are very friendly and like to chat!

The 600 seat Picture Palace closed in 1967 and is now a Grade II listed building. However there is no stopping commerce and the building is now home to a carpet shop.

This road, Oddy Street, off Tong Street, near the boundary with Birkenshaw, commemorates the Birkenshaw industrial family, the Oddys.

A retail park and other industrial units are now on the site of Shetcliffe Mill. Such out of town retail parks are today common and cater for the continual car use of today's society (sometimes at the expense of community).

This street sign designates the old Holme Lane which originally led to the hamlets of Holme and Holme Farm and Holme Wood to the West. Today it marks the boundary of the sprawling Holme Wood estate. This estate was created in the 1950s in order to eliminate supposed poor housing, to allow road widening and to create modern industrial premises along Tong Street and Sticker Lane together with other areas in Bradford. The name 'Holme' probably comes from Old English and means 'holly' and not 'home'.

'Adult' shop on Tong Street. The provision of sexual entertainment is increasingly important today, and represents changed attitudes to sexuality from those of earlier times.

This is one of the few relics of the region's extensive mining past - the Pit Hill recreation park off Holme Lane.

Photograph along Tong Street, showing land cleared of back to back (poor?) housing for road widening, which has not occurred.

This picture shows some of the council housing (made of brick not stone), which was allocated to those from the cleared housing.

This is Bowling Park Lodge, at the Lister Avenue entrance to Bowling Park. It is now a cafe.

The dominant news of the day was the Coronavirus respiratory virus, and the requirement to stay 2 metres apart (as I think is the intention of the sign!). This is 2 metres - painted on the ground in Bowling Park.

Bowling Park was purchased, from land the Bowling Iron Company used to mine for coal and iron ore in 1870. It has been attractively re-modelled as can be seen here.

Housing on Sheriden Street, Bowling. It is typical of post WW2 urban regeneration when it was thought appropriate to clear so-called slum housing (back-to-backs etc.) and build afresh.

Bolling Hall. The manor of Bolling was mentioned in the Doomsday book. Soon after that it came under the control of Ilbert de Lacy (remember him), later William Bolling and then the Tempests (of Tong Manor) held the estate until the middle of the 17th century. It then changed hands several times before being presented to Bradford Corporation in the early part of the 20th century. Since then it has been a museum to be enjoyed along with the neighbouring parkland.

This is a view of the front approach to Bolling Hall.

This is the rear view of Bolling Hall from Sheriden Street.

Bethel community church on Shetcliffe Lane was built in 1850, as part of the growing Methodist movement amongst the working people.

St John's Church on the corner of Bierley Lane and Rooley Lane was built by Dr. Richard Richardson of Bierley Hall, originally because he needed a chapel.

This is a picture of a prosperous yeoman's house on Shetcliffe Lane near Bethel church. The original timber framed house was enclosed by stone in 1625.

Here we have modern housing near to the yeoman's house in Shetcliffe Lane.

View of the road near the junction of Cutler Heights Lane and Dick Lane. The requirement to move heavy industrial equipment such as iron forgings and textiles often required large teams of horses to draw the wagons. In addition, the turning of such wagons was very space consuming. As a result, many of the roads in the district were designed to be very wide. Here we have a typical example of such a road not far from, where would have been, the Bowling Iron Works.

6 Tong and Drighlington

These two villages which are adjacent to each other, are bordering and to the West of Birkenshaw. However, they have experienced somewhat different fortunes over the years.

The first reliable mention of the Manor of Tong is as '*Tuinc*', in the Doomesday book. Again the Manor was under the ultimate ownership of Ilbert de Lacy (as a reward from William the Conqueror). The present day name probably comes from the de Tang (of Tong) family who were subsequent Lords of the Manor. As with the de Liversedges, people took their names from where they lived. The estate and Manor in its present form is attributable to the Tempest family (originating with Richard

Tempest). The remarkable feature of this area is the lack of housing and industrial development that has continued, right up to the present day. This is because, with the exception of the below the surface coal and mineral extraction by the Bowling Iron Works, the Lords of the Manor refused to allow their land to be developed in this way. With the sale of the Manor House in the 20th century to a series of owners (including Bradford University as a Hall of Residence!), the Manor is again in private (indeed business) hands and a little development is now occurring. However many vestiges of the past remain. To this day the car is not well catered for as it is difficult parking in the village, and there are many traffic calming measures.

Drighlington is mentioned in the book as '*Dreslintone*'. The word is probably from the Old English *Dryhtel* (a name) and *tun* meaning farmstead or estate. Drighlington, unlike Tong was much affected by the industrial revolution and there have been many mines, mills and industrial enterprises in the area.

The opening picture shows the main road through Drighlington.

Lumb Hall was built c1640 and may be regarded as a prosperous yeoman's residence, similar to that in Shetcliffe Lane, Bierley. Note the difference in grandeur (the house is still very grand compared with modern housing, and was by the standards of the day) compared with that of the Lord of the Manor, say Bierley Hall or Bolling Hall. In the 18th century it was lived in by James Booth, steward of the Lords of the Manor, the Tempests, at Tong Hall - we have a connection between Tong and Drighlington. His family went on to run several textile mills in the local area.

As its name suggests this is a house next to Lumb Hall which was once the Vicarage. I'm not so sure the original Vicarage would have had the electrically controlled security gates.

The first place of worship in Drighlington, was built by the then Lord of the Manor, John Sykes, in the 18th century. The present church, St. Paul's was built on the same site in 1878.

This is Drighlington's old school now converted into flats (a sign of the times). This building was constructed in 1875 and the school was originally for both boys and girls, primary and senior.

This chimney is part of what was once an over 100 year old brickworks and colliery. The buildings are now run by the successful hotel and restaurant chain - Premier Inn. It is one of several hotels serving Birkenshaw.

This building, from 1886, now the Coop supermarket, was once home to Drighlington Industrial Society. Like the Mechanics Institutes they organised education and entertainment for the working people.

Tong Leadership Academy on Westgate Hill Street is in the catchment area of Tong Manor and Holme Wood. It provides a good value education for those up to 19 years old. For example, Fulneck school in Pudsey, also in the catchment area, charges £13,000 per annum for sixth form tuition, a fee which is absent at Tong.

The gatehouse of Tong Hall, on Tong Lane - obviously rebuilt and extended. Even the gatehouse of the Lord of the Manor is substantial.

Lantern House (so called because of the lantern in the gable), Tong Lane, was believed to be tithe free (befitting a substantial house!). The red brick house next door was once The Griffin Inn.

The village inn was once The Griffin Inn. It moved to become the Greyhound Inn shown here.

St James Church, Tong, was built in its present form by, Lord of the Manor, Sir George Tempest. It is believed to be the third church on this site, superseding Saxon and Norman ones.

Home Farm is one of the newly developed enterprises in Tong. It is an off road driving centre.

Tong Farm Shop - another of the new businesses in Tong. Farmers, their margins under pressure from the processors and the supermarkets are increasingly selling their produce directly, locally, to the public.

Tong Hall is a secretive place - it is difficult to gain access up the long driveway to take a photograph. We have but a glimpse of its grandeur. In the time of the Saxons Tong Manor was cultivated by Stainulf. Like many of the region's manors ultimate control was given to Ilbert de Lacy after The Conquest. However following the 'Harrying of the North' it seems to have lain waste and untenanted. Subsequently, Asolf and his son de Tang became Lords of the Manor. The name Tong (or Tang) comes from the Old English, meaning 'fork' such as a river fork. This is because Tong lies on a ridge between two small rivers - Pudsey Beck to the North and the beck at Cockersdale to the South. The present hall was built in 1702, by Sir George Tempest, prominent Lord of the Manor.

7 Oakenshaw, Wyke, Low Moor and Wibsey

Part of the Southern tip of this area, like Birkenshaw, currently resides in Kirklees, whilst the Northern area is part of Bradford. This is an area, mostly of Bradford, which, like Dudley Hill to the West, has undergone almost unrecognisable changes.

Before industrialisation it was controlled by the great manors of the area. To the East, Bierley Hall, home of the Richardson family. Dr Richard Richardson senior was an eminent Oxford scholar, botanist and antiquarian. He is responsible for many of the ancient relics of the area. His hall has been demolished.

Part of his grounds (there is some uncertainty) have probably been used for a housing estate. Through his lands to the East, and Odsal Wood, now runs the M606 motorway spur connecting Bradford with the cross Pennine M62 motorway. Older still, to the East, Royds Hall, like Bolling Hall, mentioned in the Doomsday book. Around 1300, Royds Hall was in the possession of one of the conqueror's knight's descendants - William de Swillington.

The heavy industry caused by the advent of the industrial revolution is to be found in the South West of this area. Low Moor Iron Works and its associated mining operations, scarred both the land and the air, but was said to be a very good place to make money! (perhaps not for those working there). There were also chemical works, dye works and textile mills.

The picture is of Cleckheaton Road, looking up the hill towards Low Moor rail station.

This is the Oakenshaw War Memorial, in Victoria Park off Cleckheaton Road. Almost all communities in the area have such a memorial. Similarly there are many features, from that period, commemorating Queen Victoria.

A big, concealed house off Sal Royd Avenue. 'Royd' is a common place name and means clearing. To the West there is the large, private Royds Hall, home of successive chairmen of the Low Moor Iron Works.

The Oakenshaw cross in Wyke Lane, Oakenshaw. Thought to have been erected by Dr Richard Richardson or his family, in the 18th century, Lords of the Manor at Bierley Hall. Originally it had four sundials and a weathercock. The steps served as seats so that the villagers could gather around to discuss local matters amongst themselves. Perhaps he could have built a hall for them as he had built a church (St John's) for himself. But when you are Lord of the Manor you have a lot of freedom of action in what you do.

View of the BASF chemical plant from Cleckheaton Road. It was once a spoil heap for the Low Moor Iron Foundry. It received recent notoriety for the major fire and explosions in 1992, when being run by Allied Colloids. Next door to this on the opposite side of New Works Road there was, in the early 19th century, another chemical plant manufacturing picric acid, which was discovered to be an alternative to gunpowder in explosives. In 1916, during the Battle of the Somme, an enormous explosion at this works led to massive damage for miles around. The war was brought home.

Here we see traditional housing (over 120 years old). This is opposite the BASF plant on Cleckheaton Road.

These are traditional one storey cottages on Beacon Road, Wibsey. They are now being used as shops. 3 growth industries: a hair and beauty shop, a sandwich shop, a nail and beauty bar; and a traditional shop: a fish & chip shop.

Here we have more traditional stone housing adjacent to the High Street, Wibsey.

Wibsey Park Avenue constitutes traditional, substantial stone housing. This row of houses is opposite Wibsey Park.

This is a view of the pond in Wibsey Park.

This is a picture of Saint Andrew's Church on Cleckheaton Road, Oakenshaw. Originally Oakenshaw came under the large parish of Birstall, like many settlements in the area. This church was consecrated in 1889 and is today a listed building.

The Richardsons Arms, Oakenshaw. This is at the junction of Wyke Lane and Bradford Road. There has been an inn on this site for at least 100 years. Dr Richard Richardson, the elder, was one of Bradford's prominent gentlemen of the 17th and 18th centuries. He was an intellectual, well travelled and a scholar. In his day, he was one of the North's most eminent botanists and is thought to be responsible for bringing the Cedar of Lebanon to Bradford. His house used to lie about one mile South of the A6036 link ring road at the junction of Rockhill Lane and Bierley Lane. The house, now demolished, was until the 60's an isolation hospital. This hospital has now been replaced by a modern one further North on Bierley Lane.

Horsfall Stadium's athletics track is situated off Cemetery Road opposite the Cemetery. Currently this is the only all-weather athletics track in Bradford (a city with a population of over ½ million people). At only £3.50 for a one off use, it is an extremely good value for money way of keeping fit. The only other nearby all-weather athletics track is at Princess Mary Playing Fields in Liversedge. However Bradford always seems to have catered for the athlete - even in the early days of track and field's inception. There was an athletics track at Dudley Hill, off Cutler Heights Lane at the turn of the 20th century. In its place is now a Morrisons supermarket's distribution depot.

One of the growth industries is hotels - the Best Western Guide Post hotel, off Common Road. In front are allotments which became common towards the end of the 19th century.

Low Moor War Memorial is at the corner of Common Road and Cleckheaton Road.

One of the only remaining relics of the famous Low Moor Iron Company is this 31 ton flywheel mounted at the junction of New Works Road and Common Road. The Company itself was founded around 1790 and undertook both iron making and the mining of both coal and iron ore. Originally small, young children were needed as 'hurriers' to drag the laden coal trucks from coal seam to surface. It was hot difficult work and the men and women were often naked. Later on, in return for their labour, the Company built schools for its employees' children. The Company built much accommodation for its workers all around the site, and it expanded greatly making guns and cannon balls, then machinery and railroad tracks for the expanding industries. By 1905, three quarters of all Low Moor men worked at the site.

These are houses on New Works Road facing the foundry. It is thought that they had no windows so that the residents wouldn't be offended by the sight, sounds and smells of the blast furnaces opposite.

The Harold Club for working men was built in honour of Harold Hardy a director at the Low Moor Iron Company, by his father Gathorne Hardy. It was to honour his work for the people of Low Moor. Harold Park nearby was also given to the people.

Here is a WW1 memorial at the Harold Club.

Traditional Fish & Chip shop on Cleckheaton Road. Fish & chips are common in the area sourced from the fishing ports on the East coast. This building is thought to have once been part of a school.

This is Low Moor rail station with a Northern Line train at the platform. This is one of only two rail stations in the environs of Birkenshaw - the other being at Batley. Main stations in the area are at Bradford and Leeds. At the time of writing, the railways are making somewhat of a renaissance, as congestion by the motor car becomes more and more acute. This new station has been open since 2017.

This is a view of traditional housing by Low Moor rail station car park. Integrating the car with rail travel is sensible as is integrating developments with walking possibilities.

The George Public House, Low Moor, is situated opposite to the station. The pub is at least 100 years old.

Open spaces left by cleared housing on Lockwood Street, Low Moor, behind The George. These were often back to back houses with outside shared toilets. Improving them, strangely, did not seem to be a logistical or financial option.

The NuFarm chemical works on Wyke Lane, an Australian producer of agricultural herbicides and other products. The works was originally founded c1900, and started operations as a picric acid producer.

The Manor House on Lower Wyke Lane is hidden away. This house originates from the 17th century. It is a fairly simple house probably being the house of a wealthy yeoman, if not the Lord of the Manor. Yeomen were often freeholders with privileges such as not having to grind their corn at the Lord of the Manor's mill. The yeomen clothiers conducted business, often in rambling house like premises, subcontracting their work to others. They were the forerunners of factories.

8 References

[1] Birkenshaw - The Birch Grove, Phillip Mallpress, Pennine Printing Services Limited, 1992.
[2] History of Spen Valley, 1780 - 1980, Douglas Hird, 1985.
[3] Spen Valley Past & Present, Frank Peel, 1893, Reprint by Hardpress, 2019.
[4] Tong Hall, Tong. A History and Description of The Manor and Hall at Tong In Its Tercentenary Year, A.S. Macdonald, 2002.
[5] Gomersal - A Window On the Past, Gillian Cookson and Neil A. Cookson, Kirklees Cultural Services, 1992.
[6] The Old Halls and Manor Houses of Yorkshire, L. Ambler, 1913, p78.
[7] Birkenshaw & Oakwell Hall, 1905 (Old Ordnance Survey Maps), Alan Godfery Maps, 2014.
[8] Bradford (Dudley Hill), 1905 (Old Ordnance Survey Maps), Alan Godfrey Maps, 2013.
[9] Drighlington (W) & Westagte Hill 1905 (Old Ordnance Survey Maps), Alan Godfrey Maps, 2013.
[10] Gomersal & Birstall 1905 (Old Ordnance Survey Maps), Alan Godfrey Maps, 2004.
[11] Liversedge & North Heckmondwike 1905 (Old Ordnance Survey Maps), Alan Godfrey Maps, 2003.
[12] East Bierley, 1905 (Old Ordnance Survey Maps), Alan Godfrey Maps, 2015.
[13] Oakenshaw, Low Moor & Wyke, 1905, (Old Ordnance Survey Maps), Alan Godfrey Maps, 2015.
[14] Bradford (Odsal & Low Moor), 1905, (Old Ordnance Survey Maps), Alan Godfrey Maps, 2014.
[15] Upper Batley, 1906, (Old Ordnance Survey Maps), Alan Godfrey Maps, 2012.
[16] Heckmondwike, 1905, (Old Ordnance Survey Maps), Alan Godfrey Maps, 2005.

[17] The Bradford Antiquary, Bradford Historical and Antiquarian Society, Series 3, Vol. 4, 1989 (available online)
[18] Various online references, particularly Wikipedia.

Back cover: A picture of a garden in Birkenshaw, in November.